Text and Illustrations Copyright © 2018 Nettie Forsyth

All rights reserved.

This First Edition Published 2018.

ISBN-10: 1723570109
ISBN-13: 978-1723570100

Hare Publishing.

For Helena

Who showed me the importance of breathing.

Quotation.

"Remember to Breathe. It is after all the secret of life."

Gregory Maguire.

"When you own your own breathe, nobody can steal it away"

Anonymous

Authors Note.

This book is to help the aid of good breathing techniques in times of emotional overwhelming reactions.

To use within times of Happiness, Anger, Fear, or Sadness.

Excitement needs to have calmness just as much as that of frustration, anxiety and distress.

These breathing exercises can be fun for children to do and have life long learning benefits.

Children learn by example so please do the exercises with your children. At the time of dysregulation your children need you, your calmness and need your support.

The book needs the following materials to complete some of the tasks:
a feather, a deflated balloon, hand held mirror and a pot of blowing bubbles and a candle if you wish...

"Just Breathe"

Written and Illustrated by

Nettie Forsyth.

"Fred"...
"You are getting too worried"...
"Calm and Just Breathe" said Mum.

<u>Mirror Misting</u>

Step 1.

Have a hand held mirror to hold.

Step 2.

Take a breath in through your mouth for the count of 4

1. 2. 3. 4.

Step 3.

Pause for 2

Step 4.

Breathe out of the nose for 8 to cause misting on the mirror

1. 2. 3. 4. 5. 6. 7. 8.

Step 5.

Take a breath in through the nose for the count of 4

1. 2. 3. 4.

Step 6.

Pause for 2

Step 7.

Breathe out of the mouth for 8 to cause misting on the mirror

1. 2. 3. 4. 5. 6. 7. 8.

Step 8.

Repeat 5x

<u>Double it.</u>

Step 1.

Take a big breath in through the nose for the count of 4

1. 2. 3. 4.

Step 2.

Let a breath out of your mouth for the count of 8

1. 2. 3. 4. 5. 6. 7. 8.

Step 3.

Repeat 10 in and out breaths

Note: When starting this exercise the person may not be able to breathe in and out for the full count of 8. The out breath is double the count of the in breath.
You can progress by adding 1 more in breath to 2 more out breaths.

<u>Flower Power.</u>

Step 1.

Start with you finger in the middle of the flower

Step 2.

Take a breathe in for a count of 4 with the finger in the centre
of the flower

1. 2. 3 .4.

Step 3.

Trace your finger around the petal edge as you breathe out for
the count of 8

1. 2. .3 4. 5. 6. 7. 8.

Step 4.

Place your finger back to the flower centre and repeat the steps
2. and 3. until all the flower petal have been completed.

in

<u>I'm forever blowing bubbles</u>.

Step 1.

You will need the bubble pot and stick ready

Step 2.

Breathe in through the nose the count of 4

1. 2. 3. 4.

Step 3.

Breathe out slowly blowing through the mouth to a count of 8

into the bubble stick.

1. 2. 3. 4. 5. 6. 7. 8.

Step 4.

Pause by popping any unpopped bubbles

Step 5.

Repeat the sequence 10x

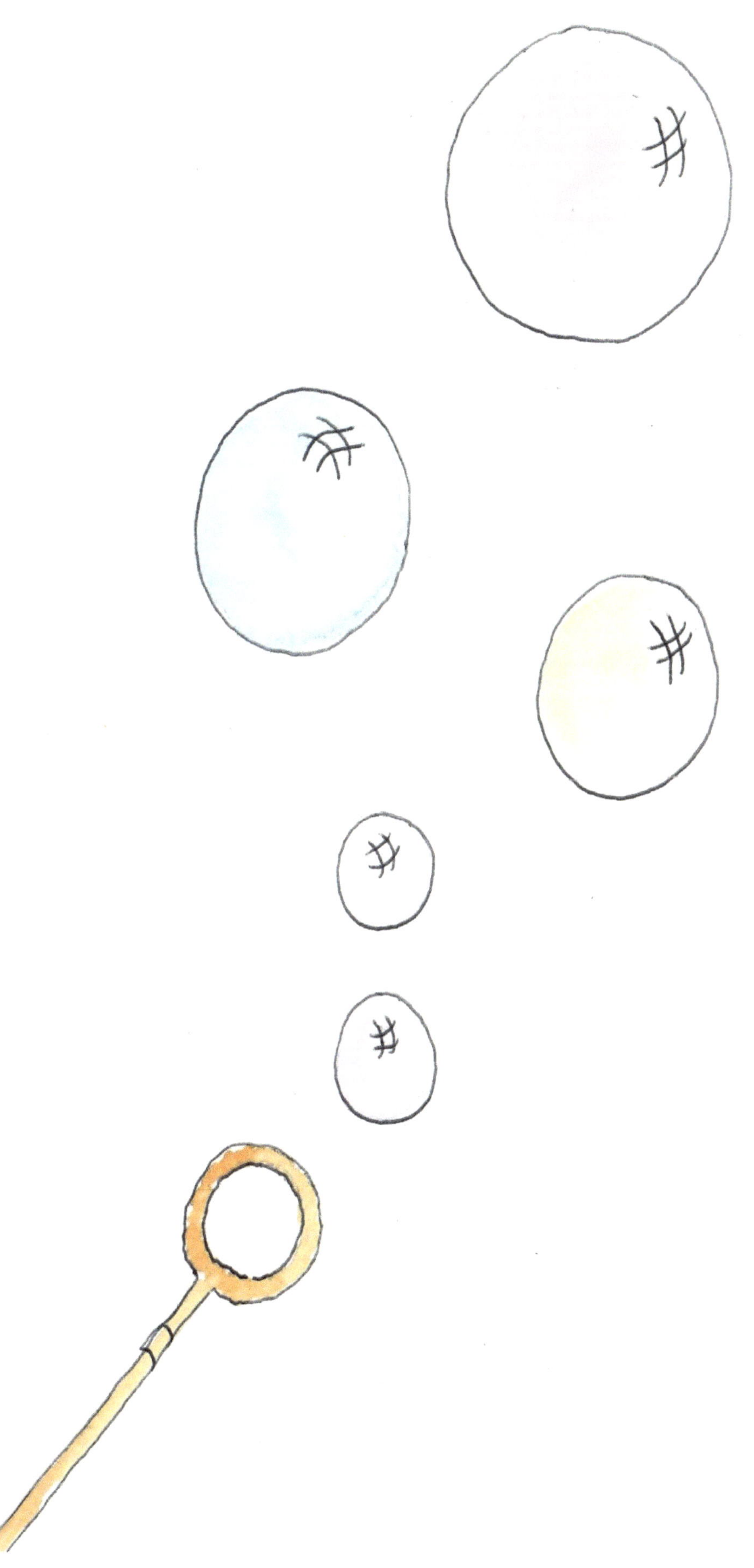

"Fred"...
"You are getting too hot"...
"Calm and Just Breathe" said Mum.

pant
pant
pant
pant

<u>Arms Up, Arms down.</u>

Step 1.

Taking the arms exaggeratedly up above the head at the same

time of taking an in breath through the mouth to the count of 4

1. 2. 3. 4..

Step 2.

Pause for 2

Step 3.

Bring down the arms slowly breathing out of the nose to the

count of 8

1. 2. 3. 4. 5. 6. 7. 8.

Step 4.

Repeat 10x

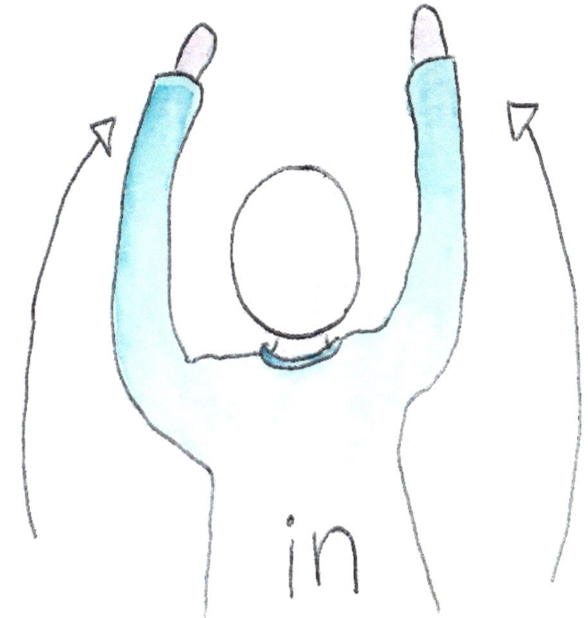
in

out

<u>Nose to Mouth, Mouth to Nose.</u>

Step 1.

Breathe in through the nose for a breathe count of 4

1. 2. 3. 4.

Step 2.

Breathe out through the mouth count of 8

1. 2. 3. 4. 5. 6. 7. 8.

Step 3.

Breathe through the mouth count of 4

1. 2. 3. 4.

Step 4.

Breathe out through the nose count of 8

1. 2. 3. 4. 5. 6. 7. 8.

Step 5.

Repeat 10x

Which is easier the mouth or the nose?

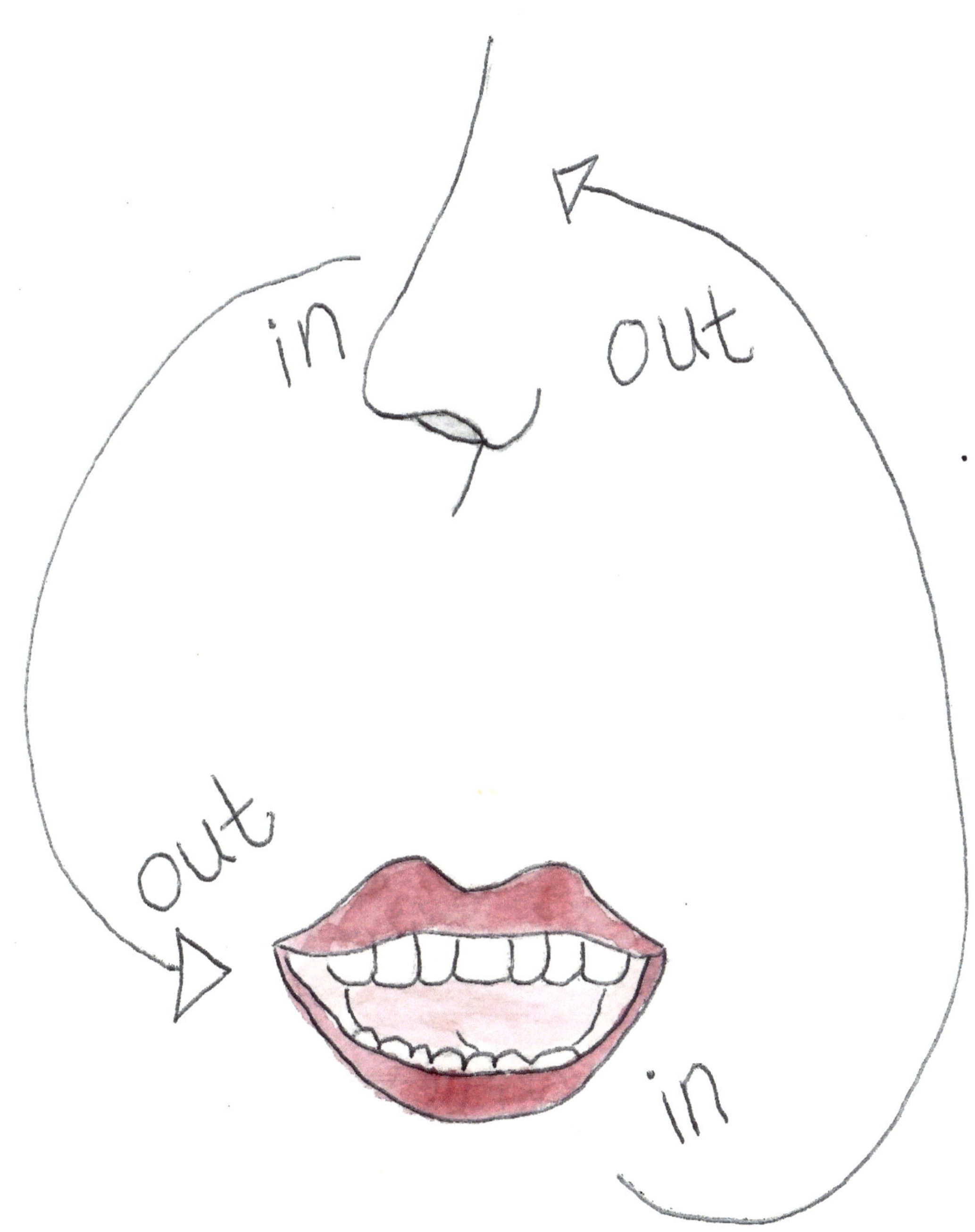
in
out
out
in

"Fred"...
You are getting too tired"...
"Calm and Just Breathe" said Mum.

zzzz
yawn
awake

<u>Thumbs up and thumbs down.</u>

Step 1.

Person puts their thumbs down to the floor as their starting

position.

Taking a breath in through the nose counting 4.

1. 2. 3. 4.

Step 3.

Breathe out through the mouth for the

count of 8 turning slowly the thumbs up towards the sky

1. 2. 3. 4. 5. 6. 7. 8.

Step 4.

Pause

Step 5.

Person repeats the sequence putting their thumbs down again

whilst taking a breath in through the nose counting 4.

1. 2. 3. 4.

Step 6.

Repeat 10x

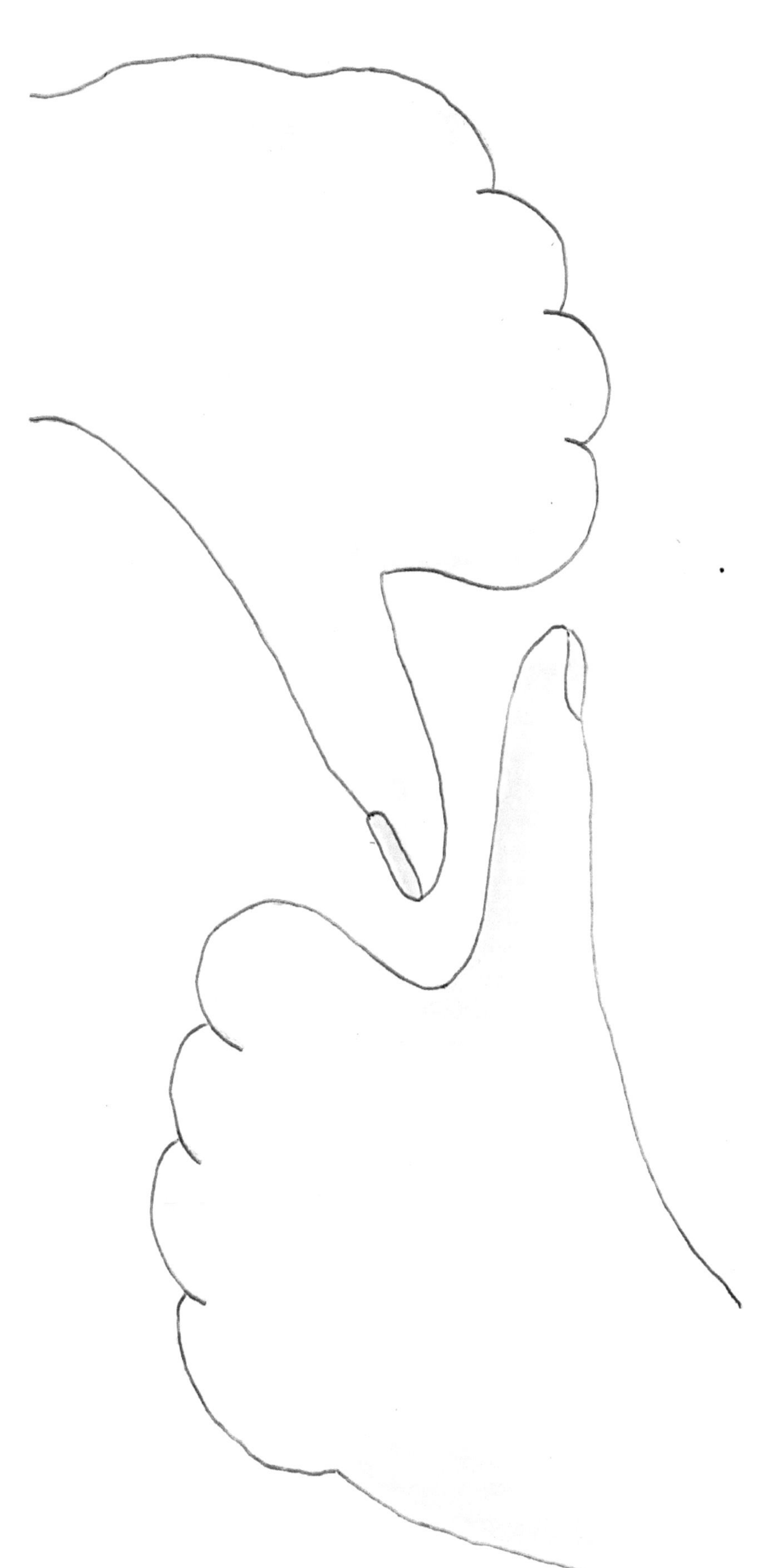

<u>Bumble Bee Hummm</u>.

Step 1.

Take a huge breath in through the nose to the minimum count

of 4 plus

1. 2. 3. 4.......

Step 2.

Breathing out in a humming sound

(mouth closed, lips together, tongue on the roof of the mouth)

until you have no breathe left.

Step 3.

Pause 2

1. 2.

Step 4.

Repeat the sequence for 10x

Note: The Hum can be loud or quiet, tuneful going up and

down the octaves.

Hummmm

Humm

mmm...mmmmm...Huummm

"Fred"...
"You are getting too upset"...
"Calm and Just Breathe" said Mum.

sob
sob
sob

<u>Balloon blow up.</u>

Step 1.

Get your balloon

Step 2.

Take a big inhale of air through the nose for the count of 4

1. 2. 3. 4.

Step 3.

Exhale the air through the mouth into the balloon for the count

of 8

1. 2. 3. 4. 5. 6. 7. 8.

Step 4.

Hold onto the balloon end. Repeat steps 2. and 3. until the

balloon is full

Step 5.

Let your balloon go, watch it whiz around the room.

Step 6.

Repeat steps 1. to 4. 5x

Step 1.

Starting in 'Pitstop' Take a breathe in to the count of 4 through the nose using the first half

1. 2. 3. 4.

Step 2.

Following the road around with the finger breathe out for the count of 8 back to 'Pitstop'

1. 2. 3. 4. 5. 6. 7. 8.

Step 3.

Repeat the second half and return to 'Pitstop'

Step 4.

Reverse using the other lane. Returning to 'Pitstop'

Step 5.

Repeat 5x

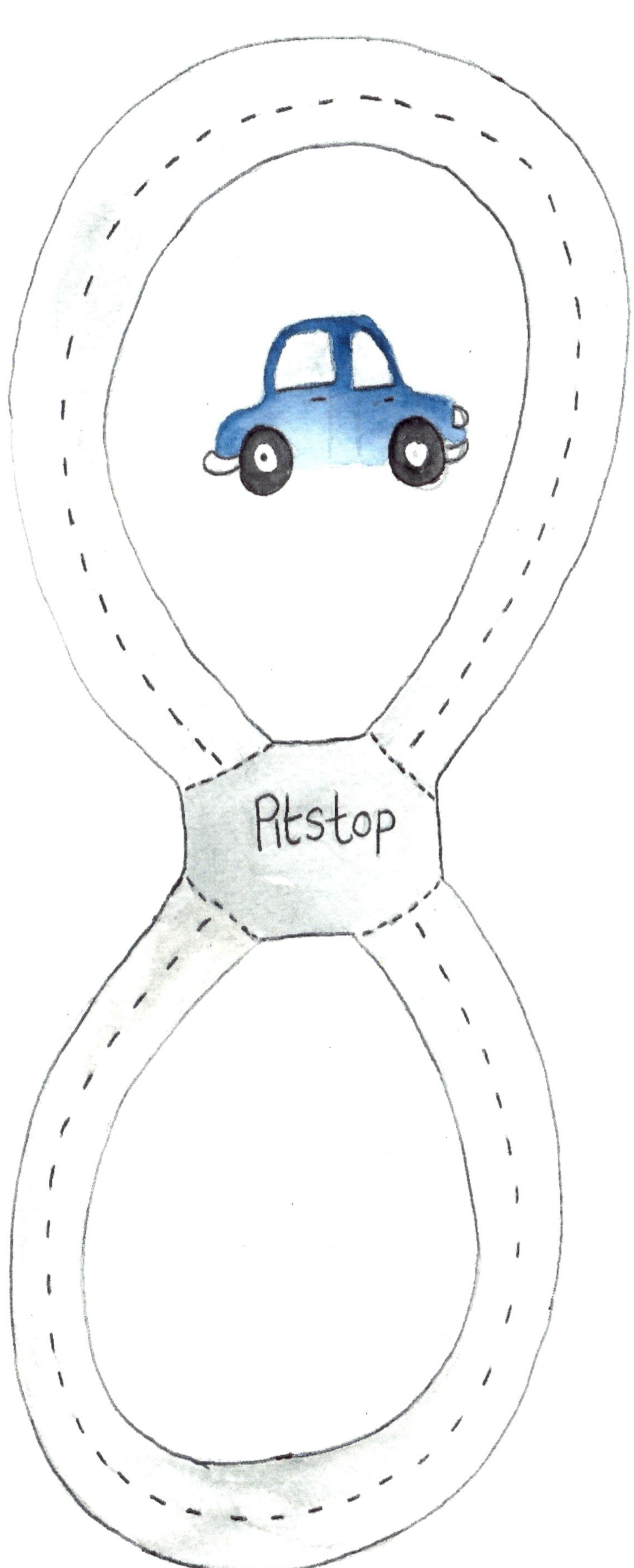

Pitstop

"Fred"...

"You are getting too angry"...

"Calm and Just Breathe" said Mum.

grr
grr

<u>Feather blow.</u>

Step 1.

Hold a light feather in the palm of the hand.

Taking a breath in through your nose for the count of 4

1. 2. 3. 4.

Step 2.

Pause for a count of 2

Step 3.

With the out breath of 8 blow it at the feather to see how far

you can get it.

1. 2. 3. 4. 5. 6. 7. 8.

Step 4.

Collect the feather and repeat 10x

Note: the feather needs to be a light wispy feather to work.

<u>Raspberries</u>.

Step 1.

Take a breath in through the nose for the count of 4

1. 2. 3. 4.

Step 2.

Blow out of the mouth with the tongue sticking out for the

count of 8 making a plaahh raspberry sound

1. 2. 3. 4. 5. 6. 7. 8.

Step 3.

Repeat steps 1 and 2 10x

<u>Steam Train</u>.

Step 1.

Breathe in through the mouth for the count of 4

1. 2. 3. 4.

Step 2.

Pause for a count of 2

1. 2.

Step 3.

Close the mouth and do quick in and out breaths out of the nose until no breath is left. The sound should sound like a steam train.

Step 4.

Repeat 10x

Note: The breath should come from the abdomen rather than the chest.

"Fred"...

"You are just too excited"...

"Calm and Just Breathe" said Mum.

yip
yip
yip

<u>Candle blow out</u>.

Step 1.

Pretending you have a candle.

Step 2

Take a breath in through the nose for the count of 4

1. 2. 3. 4.

Step 3.

Pause for a count of 2

1. 2.

Step 4.

Blow out the mouth as if you were blowing out a candle, one
big breath until there is no breath left

Step 5.

Repeat 10x

Note: A non drip real candle can be used, only with supervision.

<u>Breath Star</u>.

Step 1.

Start at the top of the star

Step 2.

Trace the finger down with the in breath through the nose to

the count of 4

1. 2. 3. 4.

Step 3.

Trace the finger slowly along to the next point to the out breath

of 8

1. 2. 3. 4. 5. 6. 7. 8.

Step 4.

Pause for a count of 2

1. 2.

Step 5.

Repeat the sequence 12x (two stars)

pause
in
out
pause
in
out
pause
in
out
pause
in
out
pause
in
out
pause
in
out

oooh
oooh
oooh

"OOH NOOO FRED"

"It's okay Mum"

"Calm down

And

JUST BREATHE"

Said Fred!

ABOUT THE AUTHOR

Nettie Forsyth is a passionate advocate of Families, Children and Child development.

Known for her simplistic but vast knowledge base of Children, Child Development, Behaviour and Emotion work.

Nettie is appreciated by many she has worked with in her therapeutic behaviour strategy and now Counselling work.

Those who have had the privilege come away as very different people enabled and empowered.

The families functions and changes have been amazing within her work, whether it be child, siblings or parents.

Her Behaviour blogs and common sense to parenting has empowered many parents.

As a parent herself got thrown into Adoption issues, Attachment, SEN and Aspergers which bought its own learning. This was used as a learning tool and gave Nettie more insight in to the world of Challenging Behaviour.

Her own Daughter becoming a successful young adult.

This all inspires the books she writes.

Contacts:

Challenging-Behaviour@hotmail.co.uk

www.help-with-challenging-behaviour.co.uk

Books Written and Illustrated by the Author.
Loveall & Spike
Just being Crab
"These things are not Okay"
Just Breathe...